THE
GREAT AMERICAN
MARBLE BOOK

by Fred Ferretti
Photographs by Jay Good

WO Workman Publishing Company, New York

First printing September 1973.

Workman Publishing Company
231 East 51st Street
New York, New York 10022.

Printed in the United States of America.

ISBN: 0-911104-27-5

With thanks to the National Executive
Committee of the National Marbles
Tournament, to the marble playing kids of
the Department of Parks and Recreation,
Yonkers, New York, to their coach, Angelo
Rauso, and to the Museum of the City of
New York.

Cover art by Chas. B. Slackman

This book is dedicated to

Gerald Rosner, Jean Colbert, Norman Horowitz, D.W. Gould, Maurice G. Steele, Oka Hester, Anne Lavelle, Linda Feldman, Tom Gallagher, Irving Perline, Cyrus Weckerle, Francis Martocci, William G. McLoughlin, William Wells Newell, Ray Jarrell, Catherine Fenzel, Robert Schonwald, Carl T. Erickson, Len Trapido, Joseph Strutt, Alice Bertha Gomme, Dorothy Howard, Rick Mawhinney, I. Benfante, Tim K. Nielsen, Clem Weinstein, Kenneth Wiggins Porter, Jerome S. Shipman, Bud Livingston, Matt Joyce, Jack Cresbaugh, Richard Harbus, Bill Sauro, Jacques Ducharme, Linda Amster, Julius Rothenberg, John B. Danby, Brian Sutton-Smith, George Springer, Elliott M. Avedon, Seymour Cohen, Margaret Whiton, Ruth E. Riley, George Maynard, Pee Wee Reese, and Donnie,

marbles players all, who shared with me their memories and skills.

CONTENTS

INTRODUCTION

IN SIMPLER TIMES, with the annual onset of Spring, the fancies of most younger men used to turn to marbles. No more.

Oh, you'll find players—kneeling, squatting and knuckling down—in America's southern, western and border states and in isolated pockets in the east, and generally they'll be arrayed around a perfectly drawn large ring shooting tournament marbles, trying to eliminate each other so that they can be local, city, state, regional or national champions. But few youngsters—boys or girls—play for fun, or for keeps, just to kill time, simply for the hell of it.

Why not?

Once-empty lots are covered with apartments and whatever space is left over is blacktopped. Alleys are concrete ramps dipping into the darkness underneath buildings. Neighborhoods no longer exist, really. Dirt is something called soil and is packed in plastic for you to buy to put in window plant boxes. Curbs are rarely seen these days. They're for parking cars or for propping up garbage cans. There is so little space, and each year there is less.

And kids' heads have changed. Marbles? What for, when there are television and statically organized Little Leagues and GP and PG movies and elaborately packaged games that reduce cosmics to throws of the dice? What for, when there are cornet lessons and tennis instruction and planned after-school peer group interactivities?

What for?

Because marbles is fun, that's what for.

And that's what—hopefully and nostalgically—this book is about, fun. And it is for all former marbles players of which there are millions; for present marbles players of which—it must be said—there are fewer; and for future marbles players. Let their tribe increase.

SOME HISTORY

IN THE UNITED STATES the varieties of marbles are virtually infinite and the game is called variously, *Ringer* or *Immies* or *Mibs* or simply *Marbles.* In England and in Scotland and Ireland it is *Taw* or *Boss* or *Span.* In Brazil children play it as *Gude;* in parts of Africa it is *Jorrah* and in Italy, *Pallina di vetro.* In West Virginia it's played with agate or glass balls. It has been played in Australia with balls of polished wood and on the streets of New York City with steel ball bearings. In Iran, Turkey and Syria it's played with balls of baked clay or with the knucklebones of sheep. Chinese chidren play at "kicking the marbles" and kids in Tasmania play at *Pyramids.*

It has been played with vigor and often excessive dedication by emperors and by overalled kids on farms shooting clay *pedabs;* by presidents and by city kids shredding their corduroy knickers as they hunkered down on cement sidewalks.

It is believed to have spawned bagatelle and the pinball machine, bowling, billiards (who will inform Minnesota Fats that he's really playing marbles?), golf, Chinese checkers and *Pachinko.*

It is an ancient game; the guess is prehistoric. Exactly where and when marbles began is not known, and the literature of marbles is skimpy and imprecise, but there do exist archaeological, anthropological and literary beacons which surface from time to time and tell us something of its origins and of its historical course.

Archaeologists have dug up small balls of clay, flint and stone in caves in Europe and in the tombs of Egyptian pharaohs. Marbles have been discovered in the digs of the Mound Builder Indians of Mississippi, and we are told that the Aztecs played a form of marbles. Pre-Christian terra cottas and other statuary often depict children playing at knucklebones and astragals, which are thought to be forerunners of marbles games. Those who have studied the beginnings of various games say that generally games began in the lower valleys of the Nile, Tigris and Euphrates rivers, spread to Africa and to Greece, thence to Sicily and to Rome, and with the Roman legions to Britain and the northern European regions and to the Germanic tribes. From Britain the movement of games coincided with the spread of empire.

According to several unattributed accounts, the suitors of Penelope are said to have rolled marbles for her hand in Ithaca while Odysseus was wandering among the Lotus Eaters; and marble enthusiasts say what David smote Goliath with was the truest of his collection of marbles. Believe it.

In *Games and Songs of American Children*, which were "collected and compared" by William Wells Newell in 1883, the game of marbles is traced to Rome. Mr. Newell wrote:

The first of these games may be descended from a sport of Roman children, mentioned by Ovid, and still in existence in which nuts are rolled down an inclined plane, with the object of striking the nut of the adversary. The second seems to be the childish reduction of a game with the ball, similar to "Golf."

The Latin expression *relinquere nuces*—putting away childish things—probably refers to that form of marbles played with polished nuts. And in *The Sports and Pastimes of the People of England*, published in 1898, Joseph Strutt wrote, "It is said of Augustus when young that by way of amusement he spent many hours in playing with little Moorish boys *cum nucibus* [with nuts]." Strutt also opines "marbles seem to have been used by the boys as substitutes for bowls, and with them they amuse themselves in many different manners. I believe nuts, round stones, or any other small things that

Boys at marbles a long time ago. This picture was photographed in the old Syrian section of New York's Lower West Side.

could be easily bowled along, were used as marbles. Those played with now seem to be of more modern invention."

Marbles was known throughout Europe in pre-Elizabethan times. In 1503 the town council of Nuremberg limited the playing of marbles games to a meadow outside of the town's limits; and in the English village of St. Gall, the town council statutes authorized the sacristan of St. Laurence to use a cat-o'-nine-tails on boys "who played at marbles under the fish stand and refused to be warned off." In France the game of *Troule-en-Madame* in which small marbles were rolled into holes at one end of a board was popular, and it moved across the English Channel to be corrupted into the children's marbles game called *Troll-My-Dame.*

Shakespeare mentions the game of *Cherry Pit* in which polished stones were tossed into holes in the ground, and in *Henry V* he talks of times when "the boys went to *span-counter* for French Crowns."

Pieter Breughel the Elder's 1560 painting "Children's

Games," which depicts about eighty of these, is regarded by historians as a prime source for information about children's games. It shows children playing marbles.

Beaumont and Fletcher in *Monsieur Thomas*, Dekker and Webster in *Northward Ho*, and John Donne in his fourth *Satire* all mention marbles games. And Richard Addison in one of his 1700 *Tatler* papers refers to "a game of marbles not unlike our common taw."

Strutt describes *Taw* as a game in which players put marbles into a ring and attempt to shoot them out "and he who obtains the most of them by beating them out of the ring is the conqueror." *Taw* was and is a community sport in many parts of England. In the Sussex village of Tinsley Green, for example, marbles, as an organized championship-style event has existed since Elizabethan times, and the village team (none of whose members is younger than 50) annually sends out blanket challenges to any team foolhardy enough to compete with them. Two hundred-year-old clay marbles are preserved by the village for its tourneys. Several years ago a crew of American sailors, christening themselves the "Swede-Bashers," were beaten by the Tinsleyites 33 marbles to 16. The captain of the Tinsley team was 86-year-old George Maynard and the star, 52-year-old Arthur Chamberlain, whose nickname is "Hydrogen Thumb."

Good Friday in England was once celebrated as "Marbles Day," a defensive ploy by the English clergy who considered a countrywide marbles day preferable to "more boisterous and mischievous enjoyments." Pubs and inns and taverns had built-in marbles "bowling alleys" for their patrons' pleasure. But there was a measure of British restraint. For university students there was no marbles playing permitted at the portals of Oxford Library; nor by law were marbles games tolerated in the Great Hall at Westminster.

In the *Traditional Games of England, Scotland and Ireland,* a book of "Tunes, Singing-Rhymes, and Methods of Playing According to the Variants Extant and Recorded in Different Parts of the Kingdom," published in London in 1894, Alice Bertha Gomme agrees that marbles had their origins "in bowls and received their name from the substance of which the bowls were formally made."

Different kinds of marbles are alleys, barios, poppo, stonies. Marrididdles are marbles made by oneself by rolling and baking common clay. By boys these are treated as spurious and are always rejected. In barter, a bary = four stonies; a common white alley = three stonies. Those with pink veins being considered best. Alleys are the most valuable and are always reserved to be used as "taws" (the marble actually used by the player). They are said to have been formally made of different coloured alabaster.

Among the marbles games played by English, Scottish and Irish children were *Boss-Out, Bridgeboard, Bun-Hole, Cob, Ho-Go, Holy Bang, Hundreds, Lag, Long-Tawl, Nine*

Holes and *Ring Taw*.

Basically, in all cultures, marbles games fall generally into three categories: chase games in which two or more players alternately shoot at each other along a makeshift meandering course; enclosure games in which marbles are shot at other marbles contained within a marked-off area; and hole games in which marbles are shot or bowled into a successive series of holes.

The English names and games crossed to this country and Americanization followed. *Picking Cherries* is after all but a variation of *Cherry Pit*, and *Ring Taw* in England is *Ringer* here; *Boss-Out* is *Follerings*, and *Lag* is *Laggers*. And other terms have been coined, to wit, *Purgy*, *Zulu Golf*, *Bounce Eye*, *Duck Taw*, *Mibs to the Wall*, *Patterson*, *Shoot the Shoe Box*, *Fat*, *Knucks* and *Skelly*. But the games are still either chase, circle or hole games, and have been played in colonial times and throughout our still-short history. George Washington was a marbles player, as were Thomas Jefferson and John Quincy Adams, and we're told that Abraham Lincoln, when he reached the age of majority and moved out of his parents' home to New Salem, became a marbles-playing terror, his specialty being *Old Bowler*. It is often a surprise to Americans to learn that marbles is not a native game, that it was played English-style in New England and in the fashion of the Netherlands in Pennsylvania.

In his *Games and Songs of American Children* William Newell talks briefly of these regional differences.

The game, when played to win the marbles of the opponent, is said to be "in earnest." If any accident happens, and the opponent's play is checked, a Georgia lad will say, "King's excuse." That this is an ancient phrase is shown by the corruption of the same cry in Pennsylvania, "King's scruse."

Newell notes that "under certain circumstances a boy who puts down a second marble is said to 'dub' (double) a marble, or to play 'dubs.'" *Dubs* is also in various parts of the country another name for *Ringer* or *Taw*.

None of our games is new, nor are they unique to this country. What are new are regional variations, with the games and the names dictated largely by the terrain. Thus in the western United States, in the south and in the southwest, where open space was and is more plentiful, the game of *Ringer*, with its 10-foot-diameter ring, became the favorite, whereas in the east, games which utilized smaller spaces and concrete sidewalks and curbs developed.

In many parts of the country, the spontaneous, unsupervised, catch-as-catch-can marbles games we once played exist only in our memories. Fewer of these "let's get up a game" marbles games seem to be played on streets and in those fields that still survive. It was with a certain sadness that one of our *Mibs* correspondents wrote to me, telling of an abortive assay into his marbles-playing childhood.

Recounting an incident that took place on a trip to Italy,

Julius Rothenberg had to say:

I did see the identical game [of Ringer] played in the rural area several miles from the Universita per Stranieri in Perugia . . . My nostalgia evoked, I tried to recall the rules as I watched, but in vain. Addressing these urchins in Italian, I asked how the game was played and what the rules were, but got the impression that there was a gap of a half-century and that I was offending their dignity and privacy in asking. And Italian kids are not generally rude. Is the game of Italian origin? Or did immigrants returning to Italy bring back the game?

Maybe.

Throughout Africa, for example, there exists a *Troll-My-Dame* type of game in which small stones are tossed rapidly and successively into a series of holes. It is called *Mancala,* and has over the years found its way to the Near and Far East. In Syria it is known as *L'ab Akila* or *La'B*

Hakimi, and along the northern Mediterranean coast it is called *Gabatta* and *Madji*. In Bali it is *Medjiwa,* in Malaysia it is called *Dakon,* and in Ceylon it is called *Chanka.* In India it is *Chongak* and in the Philippines it is *Chuncajon.* By the time it reached Australia it became *Nine Holes* and is at once similar to *Mancala,* to scores of other English "hole" marbles games and to the American marbles game of *Black Snake.*

    Nine Holes and other Australian marbles games have been studied and classified quite thoroughly by Dorothy Howard, an authority on children's games, who on a Fulbright grant looked over kids' shoulders as they shot marbles in Canberra and poured over marble lore in Perth and Melbourne. She unearthed a nineteenth-century book of childhood reminiscences by a Sir Joseph Verco called *Early Memories* which is laced heavily with his nostalgia for marbles and his joy that there were in those colonial days open spaces for marbles playing.

In those days [1860–1870] . . . the footpaths belonged to the small boys as much as to the city council, and they had no compunction in digging their "nuck" holes wherever they wanted to play, and neither the citizens nor the police ever interfered with their mining operations nor with their play.

Dorothy Howard says that with the coming of hard-packed sidewalks and pavement, concrete and macadam, hole games are disappearing and being replaced perforce by surface marbles games. She sees this as a gradual step leading to the eventual disappearance of traditional spontaneous marbles, and their replacement by standardized marbles games in international competitions.

"Perhaps," she wrote, "the time may come when an Australian child, an American child and an English child will compete in a world marble championship tournament on a space platform anchored somewhere in the wild blue yonder. In this event, this world will surely be left a dull, brave new world."

Miss Howard may perhaps be over-Huxleying it a trifle, but she appears to have a point.

"The Marble-Player" by Joseph-Louis Enderlin

AGGIES, ALLEYS AND OTHERS

THE FIRST MARBLES were fashioned from flint, stones, clay, polished nuts and wood. Through the centuries other materials came to be used, many of which have lent their names, or corruptions thereof, to the little balls.

Marbles have been made from marble, agate or lime-stone (*aggies*); alabaster (*alleys*); baked clay (*migs* or *mibs*); painted, glazed or fired clay (*clayeys, commonies, commies, kimmies* or *immies*); porcelain (*Chinees, crockies* or *potteys*); brass and iron and steel (*steelies*); glass (*glassies*); gems such as jade and turquoise and, most recently, plastic.

Generally, today's marbles are made of glass with pigments inserted for color, a continuation of the *glassie* tradition which has been credited to Venetian glassblowers. Most of these marbles come from plants in five West Virginia towns, where sand, soda ash and natural gas for firing ovens are plentiful and cheap. Master Glass in Clarksburg, Vitro-Agate of Parkersburg, Marble King of Paden City, Heaton Agate of Cairo, and Champion Agate of Pennsboro, as well as plants in central Illinois, produce an estimated 350 million marbles each year at the rate of 200 a minute.

The best consist of fresh silica and soda ash and about 20 other ingredients from aluminum hydrate to zinc oxide, a mixture which is allowed to cook for up to 18 hours at 2,300 degrees until it achieves the consistency of molasses. Once molten, it is poured down a trough that oozes it into a forming machine that makes the batter into balls. Once formed, they harden quickly and move on rollers through sizers and through an inspection process. One factory turned out 2.6 million marbles in one day and another claims it shipped 14 million marbles just for Chinese checkers games in just six months. The best marbles come from "scratch" recipes, the cheapest from reclaimed scrap glass.

Marbles are not all used by children or in parlor games. They are inserted in road sign reflectors, used in oil filters and for graining lithographic plates. Some are used as beds in fish hatcheries and others are "fried" to make costume jewelry. In this process the marbles are exposed to direct intense heat, then plunged immediately into icy water. The process leaves the surface intact but produces intricate cracks and textures inside. Marbles are useful in mausoleums where they have been found to be ideal for sliding caskets into wall crypts. They are used in pinball machines and are remelted by fabric manufacturers to create the fiberglas that is in everything from drapes to Corvette fenders. They are used as agitators in aerosol spray cans, and of course they are hoarded by collectors.

The finest marbles—of agate and limestone—still come from Germany. Today's *aggies*, regarded as the best shooters, come from Oberstein and Coburg where immense water-powered millstones round off cubes of quarried stone at the rate of about 800 an hour. Factories in Nuremberg still produce *glassies*. Germany was virtually the only major manufacturer of stone and glass marbles until about 1900, when glass marbles came under production in the United States, and then 15 years later this country began to take glass marbles manufacturing away from Germany.

The first manufactured American marbles were made of clay, and are believed to have been produced around 1884 by Samuel Dyke of Akron, Ohio; the first American company to make glass marbles in quantities was the Navarre Glass Marble and Specialty Company of Navarre, Ohio, in 1897. The company, which produced its marbles by hand, failed, reopened in Steubenville in 1902, and failed again, and it was not until 1905 when M. F. Christensen bought out the Navarre works and introduced mechanization and the assembly line that serious competition with Germany began.

Today the U.S. has the glass marbles market virtually cornered, but Germans still make the fine *aggies*. To most marbles players the *aggie* is the keystone of a collection. It is never bought, but somehow "comes" into a player's possession. Asked where his *aggie* shooter comes from, a player will say simply, "Germany, but I got it from somebody." And where did "somebody" get it? "I didn't ask."

Garrett, the 9-year-old pictured in this book, is a terror at tournament marbles and one of the kids to beat around Yonkers, New York. He got his *aggie* from his brother Ace, now 22, but still revered in Yonkers as the best marbles player you or anybody else ever saw. Garrett's *aggie* is truly a "Family Aggie." For 18 years it has bounced from brother to brother. Now it is Garrett's.

All of the kids shown shooting *mibs* with Garrett aspire

to one of the German *aggies* carried around in a cigar box by Angelo A. Rauso,their coach at the Department of Recreation in Yonkers. And where did Angelo get them? From a relative about whom he is studiously vague. It really is without taste to ask where *aggies* come from. They are simply *there*. Accept it.

"Hey, Ange, lemme have one," pleads Paulette, who, despite a self-confessed tendency to squeeze a shooter between her index finger and thumb instead of shooting *with* her thumb, in the proper manner, fancies herself one of the better shooters in Yonkers and deserving of an *aggie*. She asks Angelo again, "Please?"

"Nothing doing," teases Rauso, slamming the lid of the cigar box shut. "Not now. Sometime, maybe . . ."

Though prized by players, *aggies* do not rank as high among serious collectors. They may be rare, but are not truly scarce.

Marbles collectors are not averse to paying as much as $50.00 for mint specimens of rare marbles. Two of the more prized marbles sought by collectors are the *Lutz swirl* and the *sulphide*. The former were made between 1869 and 1888 at the Boston and Sandwich Glass Company in Cape Cod, Massachusetts. They were handmade and consisted of different colored swirls mixed with mica flecks coated with copper. The latter were made only for collectors and are really examples of bisque carvings encased in the glass of the marbles. They are rumored to have originated in China or in France, but it is known that they were made by the Chinese and exported to the United States in the nineteenth century.

They were made by taking the carved figure—usually animals, but also trains, and often children's heads—and repeatedly dipping it into the marble "batter," building up the sphere to the desired size. According to Trudy Laing in *Glass Magazine*, the most sought-after *sulphide* is one containing a bisque carving of President McKinley issued in 1901 after his assassination, and a fine example can fetch $100.00.

Another rare collectors' marble is the *Indian swirl* of black glass, made in India and never exported. Among the clay marbles prized by collectors are those from the Bennington factory in Vermont which used waste clay dipped into glaze and fired.

Of the same type are the *end-of-day* marbles of the glass factories. These were made of leftover glass by workmen, generally as prizes for their children. They were never produced for the retail market and thus are available only through other collectors.

Other kinds of glass marbles sought by collectors are the *swirled band, candy swirl, clam broth, mica, candle swirl, candy spiral, peppermint swirl, purple slag, vaseline* and of course *cleareys*. Berry Pink's small clear marbles, produced in the 1920's by the millions, are, despite their numbers, prized by collectors because of the many various colors.

According to Ms. Laing, the most notable marbles collector in our history was Thomas Jefferson, who not only was an avid player but often exhibited his finest marbles to guests.

Toe-bombsie.

A LEXICON OF MIBOLOGY

Marbles has a unique lexicon, herewith set down:

Aggies. Marbles slightly larger than usual size, most often of agate, sometimes of limestone. Most come from Germany, are heavy, and highly prized.

American fried. Larger than average marbles, of glass, that have been heated, then iced, creating inner cracks. Used as shooters.

Ante. The number of marbles agreed upon as stakes for the winner or to put into an enclosure and shot at—for keeps.

Big ring. Game similar to Ring Taw and Ringer. See Ringer.

Black beauties. Shooters usually made of obsidian or black agate. Heavy, extremely rare and prized.

Bomber. Another name for Chasing or Trailing. See Trail.

Bombsie. A rather unsophisticated arching, dropping shot.

Boss. A shooter; also short for Boss-Out, a chase game.

Bowlers. Large shooters, often aggies, often of scrap glass, but just as often reflectors pried out of traffic signs. Generally regarded as prizes because of the danger inherent in securing them.

Bowling. Rolling or throwing a shooter marble along the ground to hit a target. Bowling is generally popular with those who aren't much good at shooting. At the beginning of a game, players

often bowl to see who goes first.

Bullseye. Shooting at a hole in the ground or at the marked-off center of a designated area. Those who play it say it is a skill game; those more honest admit there's a large element of "luck."

Bumboozer. A very large marble, used as a bowling shooter. Also called a Boulder, or Caboulder or Scaboulder.

Candy stripes. Swirled red and white or red, white and blue marbles. Prized early German glassies.

Cats eyes. Glass marbles with football-shaped wedges of color in otherwise clear glass.

Chase games. Basically a game in which players chase one another's marble, trying to hit the opponent's, thereby winning it. Chase games neither call for enclosures—rings, squares, triangles—nor holes or pots. For variations of the game, see Boss-Out (page 65) and Chasies (page 66).

Clams. Marbles.

Clayeys. Small marbles of clay. Never used as shooters but rather as target or object marbles. Held in low esteem.

Clearance! A defensive shout which permits one to clear away roughness or debris before shooting. Such a shout negates a possible "Smoothie" penalty. See Smoothing.

Cleareys. Clear glass marbles, often tinted and bubbly inside.

Clodknockers. Ordinary marbles to be shot at. See Mibs.

Commies. Pronounced "Come-ee" not "Commie" as in "Commie Rat." The small marbles at which shooters are shot. See Mibs.

Commons. See Commies.

Crockies. See Commies.

Cunny thumb. To shoot with the knuckles off the ground.

Regarded as a "sissy" way of shooting.

Dibs. Clay marbles, clayeys.

Doughies. Another name for clayeys.

Dubs. Hitting two or more marbles out of a ring with one shot. The caroms involved make this one of the prettiest shots in championship play. Also used as another name for Ringer.

Ducks. Object marbles, to be shot at.

Edgers. Marbles near the edge of the ring.

Eggies. Short for "Can I borrow a few marbles?" as in "Eggies on the aggies?"

Enclosure games. Also called circle games. Games in which marbles are shot within a confined area outlined on the ground. The shapes are usually geometric, most often a circle or a square. For variations of the game, see Ringer (page 91) and Knuckle Box (page 107).

English. To give the shooting marble backspin, causing the target marble to carom off in unexpected directions.

Eye drops. Dropping a shooter directly down on an object marble. A "luck" shot.

Fens! Or Fins! or Finns! An all-inclusive call by which a player can suspend all rules until he has planned his shot. A most valuable offensive ploy.

Flints. Another name for aggies.

For fair. Playing only for the results of a game. All of the marbles won are returned, either to their owner or to the tournament.

For keeps. For keeps.

Fudging. Easing your hand over the ring line before shooting. In tournament play this is cheating and carries a one-shot forfeit. Also used as a general term for cheating.

Glancing shot. A shot not head on, that hits the target tangentially, then bounces off.

Glassies. Glass marbles. Larger ones are used as shooters.

Globolla. Giant glass marble used in bowling games.

Heggies. See Eggies.

Heist. To rest one's shooting hand atop the other hand. Before shooting, a call of "Heist!" is necessary. A call of "No Heist!" by another player means one is out of luck.

Histing. Raising the hand from the ground before shooting. This is cheating.

Hit. When a marble is knocked out of a ring.

Hole. Also called pot. Holes in marbles games can vary in depth—from the size of a twelve-year-old's heel to something dug out with a garden spade. Shallow holes are called saucers.

Hole games. Games in which the object is to get marbles in a hole, out of a hole, a certain distance from a hole—always a hole. For variations of the game, see Potty (page 72) and Nucks (page 83).

Hoodles. Object marbles, to be shot at.

Hunching. Moving the hand forward while shooting. This is cheating too. In tournament play this means inching one's hand over the edge of the ring. Also known as fudging, and carries a one-shot penalty.

Immies. Imitation agate. Initially of clay, later of ordinary glass. In Canada, milky marbles to be shot at, or in a pinch, used as substitute shooters. In eastern United States, a general term for all marbles games.

Inching. See Hunching.

Jumbos. See Globollas and Bowlers. Also called Caboulders.

Knuckle down. To rest one or more of one's knuckles on the ground while shooting. A general term denoting the correct form for shooting. The marble should rest against the ball of the first finger rather than in the crook.

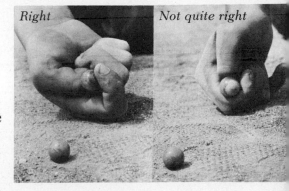

Right *Not quite right*

Knucks down tight. Ditto.

Lagging. The act of tossing or shooting from the Pitch Line. Whoever comes closest to the lag line without going over it shoots first. See Pitch Line.

Lag line. A straight line tangent to, and touching, the ring in tournament play.

Little solids. Small glass marbles, solid color. Used as target marbles. The marbles in Chinese checkers sets.

Lofting. The act of shooting a marble through the air in an arc to hit a marble in the ring. Also called Popping.

Marker. A single marble used as a target.

Marrididdles. Homemade clayeys.

Mibs. Object or target marbles. Also Mibbies, Mibsies, Miggs, and Miggles.

Milkies. Translucent white glassies.

Miss. When player fails to knock an object marble from the ring.

Monnies. Another term for shooters.

Moonaggies. Marbles made of carnelian. So named because when they crack, generally from the inside, moon or crescent shapes form on the surfaces. A cure for the cracks is complete submersion in grease or lard.

Pedab. Another name for Doughie.

Peeries. Small clear glass marbles. Often used as another name for cleareys.

Peewee. A very small marble.

Pitch line. A straight line opposite from and parallel with the Lag Line.

Plumpers. See Trail.

Pot. See Hole.

Pot marble. Another name for Little Solids.

Potsies. Another name for Ringer.

Potty. Circular hole dug into the ground, into which marbles are shot.

Puggy. Game in which marbles are shot into the Potty.

Purgy. See Ringer.

Purey. Small clear glass marbles, brightly colored. Highly prized and generally worth from two to five clayeys.

Rainbow mibs. Target marbles.

Rainbow reeler. A multi-colored shooter.

Realies. Real marble marbles, as opposed to glass. Thought to be another name for moonaggies.

Ringer. The "official" marbles game as played in the National Marbles Tournament. It is played by placing 13 marbles in the form of a cross in the middle of a 10-foot-diameter ring. Shooters shoot from the ring's edge and knock marbles out of the ring. The first player scoring seven hits wins.

Ring taw. Another name for Ringer.

Rollsies! A defensive call to force a player to roll his shooter in a bowling marbles game rather than throw it.

Roundsters. Circling around the playing ring, seeking the best shooting position. Also called Rounders.

Scaboulder. See Globolla.

Scrapper. A glass marble made from scrap glass. Some Bowlers are Scrappers.

Scrumpy knuckle. To shoot with the knuckles off the ground. Another name for Cunny Thumb.

Shooter. The agate marble shot at other marbles. Generally slightly larger than the ordinary run of glassies. Most are made in Germany and appear to find their way here by osmosis.

Shooting. Also called firing, flicking, pinching, dribbling, pinking, dribbying, drizzying, throwing or bowling. See Knuckle Down.

Shot. Snapping the marble from the hand with the thumb from where it is held against the ball of the first finger. Knucks, of course, must be down.

Smokies. Glassies with puffs of color inside.

Smoothing. Leveling off, removing obstacles from the ground before shooting. Forbidden, and carries a one-shot penalty.

Slip. Misplay when marble falls from the hand. Player reshoots.

Snooger. A near miss.

Solid peewees. Term for the 13 marbles in the center of the championship ring.

Spannies. A shooting distance. The measurement between the tip of the thumb to the tip of the middle finger when stretched apart.

Steeley. Usually a ball bearing. Popular as a shooter in the World War II era. It helped to have a father who worked in a defense plant.

Stick. When a shooter's marble stops inside the ring after knocking a target marble out of the ring. The shooter may shoot continually if he continues to stick.

Sticker. Object or target marble.

Sugar. To rough up a shooter either on concrete or with sandpaper to afford oneself a better grip.

Taw. Another name for a shooter.

Three-finger-flat. Player shoots with the thumb and first finger while keeping his three other fingers flat to the ground.

Throwsies. Common sort of shooting in bowling-type games.

Toe-bombsie. Using the toe height to shoot from in bowling games. Very expert, achieves bouncing caroms.

Trail. General term for marbles games in which shooters follow each other as they move from one location to another. Also known as Chasing, Plumpers, and scores of other names.

Walk. As in "Take a Walk." When a player walks through the ring in a match. He must give up one of the marbles he has won if he does this.

Waters. Clear glass marbles.

Zebras. Glass marbles with white and black swirls. Common in New York City, rare elsewhere. Prized as shooters.

Zulu golf. One of many terms for games in which players shoot into a series of holes dug into the ground.

OPINIONS ON TECHNIQUE

WHEN I EMBARKED upon this book I knew how to play marbles. Of course I did. You drew a circle or a square in the dirt, then you and your fellow players dropped in your antes and, in turn, shot at them, winning those you were able to displace from the drawn boundary lines. Right? Wrong.

The varieties of marbles games are infinite and the techniques used in playing them are various. Marbles games through the years have generally fallen into the three categories we described—the chase, the hole and the circle or enclosure. But refinements and ingenious adaptations have been created in different countries, even in different neighborhoods, and in different times. How big should the circle be? Or the square? When shooting at or into a cup dug into the ground, should one shoot knuckles down or simply bowl? Should the hole be deep or shallow? Dug out or fashioned with the heel of a boot or a shoe or a sneaker? Why in one game are holes measured precise distances apart and in others placed willy nilly? The rules for tournament marbles are rigorously prescribed, written down, and policed and yet for similar nontournament games they are amorphous and freewheeling. Why?

The answers are difficult to arrive at. Marbles literature is woefully weak on historical lore; one man's rules are another's discards, and structure in Surrey is ridiculous in Wheeling. The best explanation I can come up with is usage. Games are played one way in one place simply because they have always been played that way in that place. Clear? Of course not, but valid nevertheless. The games of marbles have historical roots, and the similarities among the types of games —chase, hole, and circle games—are not to be denied, but in the actual playing, substantial differences arise.

The correct way of shooting, tournament marbles dictates, is to place all of the knuckles (save the thumb) on

Good   Not so good

the ground, place the shooting marble inside the first finger between the tip and the first joint, and secure it there tightly with the tip and nail of the thumb. The marble is propelled by the thumb forcibly ejecting it from its nesting place.

But other games suggest that one can shoot without one's knuckles being grounded, or with but one or two knuckles to the ground. Others dictate that marbles be shot from several feet above the ground. It is also true that placement of the knuckles and the height from which shooters are propelled make marbles do different things.

Slanting the hand forward and bearing down heavily on your first knuckle when shooting will generally cause a shooter to spin backward, or spin in place after striking a target marble. A player will aim carefully for one side of a target marble or the other, and a successful hit can cause the shooting marble to carom considerable distances in either direction, if that is the player's wish. Shooting from above ground level will invariably force the shooting marble to bounce only a short distance from the spot of impact. Just as in billiards, "English" can be obtained, but with marbles it is the thumb that acts as the cue tip—under the marble for backspin, toward the top for the reverse.

Body position is dictated by the lay of the game. If a shooter is near enough for dead-on aim, he more than likely will get down in a prone position, dig his chin into the ground, close one eye, aim and shoot. Others shoot on bended knee; others hunkered down on one side of their bodies; others from a crouch or a squat.

In theory it would appear that the stricter rules apply generally to games which I like to call shooters' or gamblers' games, that is, the circle games. In these—though one might be playing with a friend—the aim is to wipe him out, take all his marbles, drub him, defeat him, humble him, send him home without his shooter. It's war in agate, and naturally one doesn't give an inch here, a relaxation of rules there. That's not done. On the other hand, in chase games and hole games particularly, the object is either fun or simply killing time. Often marbles are won but just as often these games are played for simple enjoyment.

Common to all marbles games are a few general conventions. In all types of games, hole, chase or circle, a player who fails to achieve his objective—either to get into a hole or to hit another player—has to yield his turn to the next player. In hole games, a player who gets his marble into the hole is allowed to take it out and place it on the lip of the hole for the next shot in the game. Another "understanding": generally the shooting line is used only for the first shots.

There are basically two general types of marbles—those that are hit and those that are used as hitters. The former can be anything from clay *pedabs* to *glassies;* the latter are either pure agate marbles or, for those who lean toward bullishness, steel ball bearings.

Often geography and environment influence games. A city dweller who happens to be an expert shooter can forage off his block looking (like Minnesota Fats) for action, and almost invariably will play "for keeps" with some fellows he may never see again. On the other hand, in rural regions or suburban neighborhoods, marbles players—like people in general—are more scarce, more familiar and, given the underlying awareness that one most probably will have to play over and over again with the same players, their tendency is to be more relaxed, less competitive, to play more often "for fun" or "for fair."

Of course when you play with the same people repeatedly, and lose repeatedly, the sometime humiliation of losing becomes pure shame. Who would not long for anonymity then? Listen to a loser (notice, by the way, that he declines the use of his name):

"When I was a kid, the worst shame I could possibly feel happened when I ran out of marbles. That meant that not only had I not won any lately, but also that I had been losing my inventory. The only thing to do at that point was to go to a toy store and buy some. Can you *believe* that? A *toy* store? I would have been disgraced if anyone had seen me doing that. So I used to get on a bus and travel to a toy store in the next town where nobody knew me. I was like some sort of hired gun—arriving in town for some dark, secret purpose."

But most players were not losers always. They won a little, lost a few, had winning streaks and days when every straight-on shot seemed, radarlike, to veer into off-course pebbles. It happens, and the best players are those who can accept both good days and bad with equanimity.

Actually much of the effort in marbles games is devoted to making up and enforcing the ad hoc regulations devised for the various games.

Why this kind of layout, this depth of hole, this length of lag line, this shooting distance? The temptation is to dig too much and one finds oneself getting overly involved with speculative theory and, perhaps, spurious analysis of techniques. One finds oneself ascribing more meaning to marbles than one ought to. So I'll shut up and just say enjoy!

Here are some of the ways you can.

GAMES

Boss-out

This appears to be the oldest marbles game as well as the oldest chase game, identical, it would appear, to that mentioned by Ovid and played by Augustus. It is described in Strutt as "a game at marbles" in which "one bowls a marble to any distance, which serves as a mark for his antagonist to bowl at, whose business it is to hit the marble first bowled, or lay his own near enough to it for him to span the space between them [i.e. a hand's span between them] and touch both the marbles." [*] No specific distances are mentioned. If the antagonist can't hit the target marble or span to it, the roles change and he, the chaser, becomes the chased.

[*] Joseph Strutt, *The Sports and Pastimes of the People of England* (London, 1898).

In Great Britain, since Elizabethan times, it has also been known as BOSS AND SPAN, and a variation of it in which penalties of one marble are assessed for each hit is called LONG-TAWL.

In Australia it is FOLLOW-ME-TAW, FOLLOW, BLACK TRACK, TRACK TAWS, TRACTOR KELLY, TRACTOR TAW and KISS AND SPAN.

In the United States it is called CHASIES but is also known as TRAILS or TRAILING, BOMBER, CURB, SPAN and, in Massachusetts, PLUMPERS.

Chasies In the American version of BOSS-OUT
the player who hits or spans to his opponent's marble takes that marble. Then, as the winner, he tosses his own marble ahead. However, if the distance between the marbles is less than a step but more than a span, the shooter has the option

(always exercised because of the variety it offers) of picking his marble up and dropping it straight down from face level in an attempt to hit his opponent's marble. This is called BOMBER.

A Connecticut variation involves setting stakes of several marbles per hit, but this requires extensive bookkeeping. In New York the players once used curbs as guides for their throws; in Toronto EYE DROPS replaced BOMBER; and in Iowa it became BOMBSIES.

Unless multiple stakes are agreed upon, this game involves little exchange of marbles but consumes enormous amounts of time. It is also a game which demands use of one's best shooter—an *aggie* or a *steelie*. It is wise to keep an adequate supply of ordinary *immies* in one's pocket so that the possibility of having to pay a debt with one's shooter be avoided.

Holilakes

This was the earliest English hole game. A hole was dug into the ground and the competition was to see who could toss or roll his marble in first. Intricate hole games evolved from this, such as HOLY BANG.

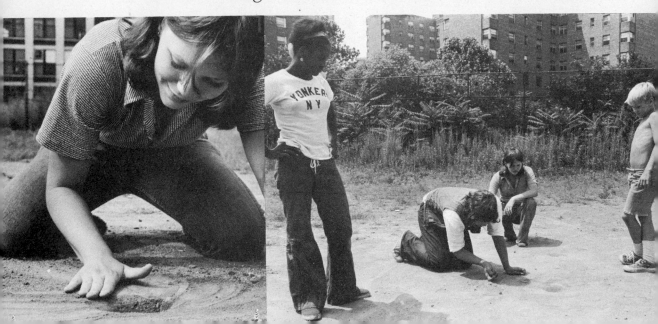

Holy bang

Place a marble in a dug out hole as a target. The first player able to get his marble into the hole and so hit the target marble three times is the winner and collects all of the missed marbles tossed in the game.

HOLILAKES also spawned COB, a game in which several players bowl their marbles into a series of four holes in the ground (see ROLLY-POLLY).

The varieties of hole games are endless, with specific rules being laid down for games of one, two, three, four or more holes, and such refinements being advanced as the sort of hole to be dug.

An ideal hole slopes smoothly into the ground at an angle of about 45 degrees, and curves gently to the opposite slope. There should be no lip.

Good

Not so good

Hundreds

This is another simple one-hole English game for two players. A hole is dug and a shooting line is drawn from eight to 15 feet. The players attempt to get their marbles into the hole. A player getting his shooter or *boss* in the hole receives 10 points, and has the option of either going back to the line for another shot at the hole or shooting at his opponent. A hit also counts 10 points. A person hitting another gains 10, but the one hit also loses 10, thus achieving 100 points can be a difficult and lengthy venture.

Bun-hole

A hole in the ground is scooped out in the shape of a saucer, not deep but slightly concave, and marbles are shot at it from a shooting line about eight to 15 feet away. If more than one hole is used the game becomes HOLY BUN-HOLE.

These basic one-hole games have traveled. BUN-HOLE in England is BUNNY-IN-THE-HOLE in New England, and in Australia it is BASINS, BUNNY HOLE, IN THE HOLE, HOLEY and GOOT.

In the American midwest it is called BULLSEYE, in Pennsylvania PUGGY and up in New Hampshire it inspired a marbles game as winter sport, LAST CLAMS.

Potty

This more intricate one-hole game had its heyday in the New York City borough of Queens because it required the kind of dirt driveway with which Queens once abounded. In time, the dirt driveway gave way to the alley.

The hole or "potty" is dug seven or more feet from the shooting line. Players throw their marbles toward the potty, the closest throw winning first shot. The object of the game is to get into the potty but not to get too close if you fail. Being in the potty entitles the advantaged to "spannies," that is, he can keep all the marbles that are a hand's span from the lip of the potty.

POTTY is a double-edged game. Though it's desirable to get into the potty (as you can help yourself to any marble that comes too close), once in it, you are at the mercy of the next person who follows you in. That person has three chances to knock you out of the pot and thus take your marble. If he fails, you have three chances to hit him. You can make it hard for someone to shoot your marble out of the potty by substituting a tiny *peewee* in its place. On the other hand, the attacker can substitute an oversized *scalboulder* (see A Lexicon of Mibology) in an attempt at brute force.

A thinking man's game. It is good/bad to be the first into the potty. It is good/bad to be quite close to the potty. Strategies and measurements tax the mind in this "ruthless" game.

Pot In this New Jersey variation of POTTY, players put up stakes of marbles in a circle around the pot. Once a player gets his shooter into the pot, he can put it on the lip and shoot at the stake, keeping any marble he shoots off the circular ring. A game for only the best shooters.

Another New Jersey variation, also called POT, specifies that once having gotten into the pot, a shooter take his marble out to the lip of the pot and try to shoot an opponent from there.

This requires some elementary knowledge of pool hall "English" and strong, propelling knuckles. Only for the strong.

Puggy

Like POTTY, this is a hole game, but there the resemblance ends. First, the hole has to be dug with the heel of a shoe and to a depth of that heel. Then the players stand upright about six inches from the hole and, at random, drop whatever stake of marbles is decided upon, usually three. The players then shoot from a shooting line about ten feet away and attempt to propel these target marbles into the hole or "puggy." A player continues shooting until he misses; an expert shooter could conceivably—like a good pool player—run all of the marbles.

This rarely happened in Scranton, Pennsylvania, where PUGGY was regarded as a "girls only" game, and it was common knowledge that girls weren't good shooters.

In Yonkers, in New York's Westchester County, the players gathered in a circle around the hole or pot. They shot for the hole and if successful became "killers," eligible to go after the marbles of others. A stake of several marbles was agreed upon for each hit.

Killer

In Brooklyn, PUGGY was simply called KILLER. Players, after shooting at the hole from a line a dozen feet away, shot at their opponents' marbles. The extra added attraction here was that one played "for keeps" for *aggies*, the favored shooters. This was a tense business. Only the best shooters played KILLER.

Newark killer Another

"strictly for shooters" game is native to Newark. In this one
the players begin by tossing their shooters into a hole about
eight feet away. After successfully entering the hole, the
player can then shoot at an opponent's marble. If it is
hit, that player is not only eliminated from the game but also
loses his shooter *and* pays a bounty of one or more marbles.

The successful shooter has the option, after hitting one
player, to aim at another by either placing his shooter on the
lip of the hole and shooting from there or by shooting from
where his marble lays. This is the toughest of the one-on-one
shooting games, and those who played it were the neighborhood's top guns. The best thought so highly of themselves
that they refused to recognize the annual winner of the
National Marbles Tournament because the competition
didn't involve a pot.

Last clams

Marbles as a winter sport; a New Hampshire game, as one might expect. Dig a hole at the base of a snow bank, taking great care to see that the hole, the depth of a galosh heel, is packed tightly. Make an icy rim by tamping with warm hands.

The marbles are here considered "clams," and the first person to shout "Last Clams!" goes last and has an obvious advantage, soon to be seen.

A point is marked off about 12 feet from the hole. From here, the first person tosses his clam toward the hole, drops it in the snow wherever he likes, or with his finger etches an arm's length trench in the snow in the general direction of the hole and rolls his marble toward it. He could, if daring or confident, dig a trench all the way to the hole and toss his marble down it. The danger of using the trench is that once the marble comes to rest it is at the mercy of the last shooter, who can shoot for the hole or at any other marble. A marble in a trench is easy prey. If he hits a marble he receives a one-shot bonus and can conceivably work his way to the hole on the backs of the other players. On the other hand he too can elect to weave his way to the hole via a trench.

A mass of trenches criss-cross their way toward the hole, each player inching forward but being careful not to be belted out of contention. Hitting an opponent entitles the aggressor to a free shot with which to further his trench.

The game was generally played with mittens, hands cupped, palm upward, using the knuckle of the index finger to propel the shooter. Crucial shots were, of course, taken barehanded, regardless of the cold. Cold hands a small price to pay for being the winning clam.

LAST CLAMS appears to be the only instance on record of marbles as a winter sport. It is generally regarded as a spring pastime, beginning with the soft ground that comes after winter. However, games *have* been known to be played in mud or slush.

Nucks

There seem to be no two-hole marbles games, but there are a few three-holers. One of these, an Australian game, calls for three saucer-shaped and -sized holes, each a yard apart. Players begin from a shooting line about ten feet away from the first hole, and shoot for the first, second and then third. A player can keep shooting as long as he's landing his marble in the saucers. When he misses, the next player gets his turn. The second has the option of shooting for a saucer or "kissing" his opponent off the track, for which he wins an extra shot. The first player to traverse the three holes three times is the winner.

Sir Joseph Verco in *Early Memories* wrote, "It had to be played necessarily kneeling down, and not otherwise, and so tended to produce a definite bagging of the trousers at the knees, and the wearing of holes there, as well as an accumulation of dirt and even of abrasion at the knuckles of the hands."

Spanning

This is a Long Island version of NUCKS. In it, the holes are shaped like pots instead of saucers. As with NUCKS, a player has the option of either shooting for a pot or shooting at an opponent's marble. If he hits the latter, he receives an extra shot.

Once in a hole, a player can span out from its lip (by stretching his hand from thumb to forefinger) and shoot from there.

The first player through the three holes can shoot at his opponent's with the power to eliminate those he hits. A player who is eliminated has to pay a stake of marbles— usually five or six, or a number agreed upon before the game.

The shooting line in this game—from which all players start—is at least 20 feet from the first hole, a sizable distance that makes this difficult game more difficult. Instead of a yard between saucers, as in the Australian version, there are 10 feet. For good shooters.

Poison

There are several four-hole games that generally involve moving from hole to hole in order. These appear to be played in England, Scotland, Ireland and in Australia, and include CASTLES, POT HOLES, HOLES, POISON and BASINS. But in one of these, POISON, there is an interesting variation.

Four holes are dug, three in a line and a fourth about five feet to the side of the third. Players must go from the first to the second to the third; back to the first; and again, from the first through the third, and *then* into the fourth or Poison hole. He then becomes "Poison" and may shoot at the marble of any other player, and claim it, or an agreed upon stake, if he hits it.

Rolly-polly

This five-hole marbles game was popular in the Philadelphia-Central New Jersey area. Five holes, up to four inches deep, are dug in a line, three feet apart. The players shoot from a starting line about 10 feet from the first hole and make their way through the five holes. Once through they become "Killer" or "Poison" and can shoot their fellow players out of the game.

Da bawh ji

A southern Chinese six-hole game for which five holes are arranged pentagonally, with a sixth in the middle. The winner is he who gets his marble through the five outer holes (counter-clockwise) and into the center hole. Landing in a hole entitles the advantaged to another turn. The marble is removed from the hole and shot from the lip.

A player may shoot his opponents' marbles away from the holes as he goes along, receiving an extra shot for a hit.

Black snake

This is an American seven-hole game. The holes are dug at irregular and unmeasured intervals. Players must progress through all seven holes, then return back through the holes to become "Black Snakes." Attaining that distinction, a player is entitled to shoot at other players' marbles. Once hit, a player is eliminated from the game. However a "Black Snake" must be careful too; if he shoots into any of the seven holes *he* is eliminated.

Generally no marbles are at stake. The game is played only with shooters and is looked upon as a kind of championship scrimmage, an excellent opportunity to develop aim and backspin.

This game was popular in Ohio and Kansas and throughout the midwest, and was only, obviously, for the best of shooters.

Nine holes

An English game, a derivative of golf. Nine holes are dug into the ground, either in a squared or rounded S-shape, and the players shoot into them in turn, one at a time. The players do not shoot at each other and the winner is he who, according to Strutt, "completes in the fewest bowls" the nine-hole course. According to Strutt this was a most popular game in nineteenth century London.*

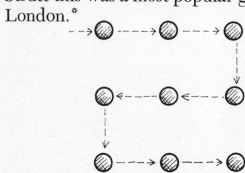

* Joseph Strutt, *Sports and Pastimes of the People of England* (London, 1898).

Poison hole

Poison hole is similar to nine holes but is played on a course of 11. Though its name connotes a "Killer" or "Poison" type game, it is essentially a form of golf.

Ringer

The circular game of RINGER, played in the national championships, is the most complicated of the circle games. A circle 10 feet in diameter is marked off (in Wildwood where the tournament is held permanent circles are painted on concrete blocks, buried beneath the sandy beach most of the year and uncovered only at tournament time in June). Thirteen marbles are placed in the center of this circle in the shape of a cross. The winner is the player who is the first to shoot seven marbles out of the ring. The eliminations are held over a week with players competing against each other on a round-robin basis. The finalists are, of course, those who win the most games in the round robin. (Detailed rules can be found on pages 138–147.)

Lag RINGER is merely a sophisticated derivative of LAG in which, according to Addy's *Sheffield Diary*, "A number of boys put marbles in a ring, and then they all bowl at the ring. The one who gets nearest has the first shot at the marbles. He has the option of either 'knuckling doon' and shooting at the ring from the prescribed mark, or 'ligging up' [lying up]—that is, putting his *taw* [marble] so near the ring that if the others miss his *taw*, or miss the marbles in the ring, he has the game all to himself next time. If, however, he is hit by the others, he is said to be 'killed.' " Much of the strategy lay in positioning the marbles.

Circle games abound. In England they are TAW as well as LAG and RING TAW. In Australia they are called THE RING, CIRCLE, BIG RING, LITTLE RING, BIG CIRCLE, LITTLE CIRCLE, as well as JUMBO, POISON RING and EYE DROP. In the United States they are known as RINGER and RING, as POTSIES and DUBS, and in Italy as PALLINA DI VETRO. All of the games involve putting marbles in a ring and then shooting them out.

There are even half-circle games known as HALF MOON, TOWNSEY and MOONEY TED FIRST.

Potsies

This is probably the most universal of circle games. It is also called DUBS or 25-A-DUB or 100-A-DUB. Each player contributes a given number of marbles to the "pot," which is a large ring drawn on the ground. These are arranged in cross-fashion or in the form of a circle. The player who bowls closest to the ring goes first.

The object is to knock marbles out of the ring while keeping one's own shooter *inside*. If the shooter goes outside the next player plays. The first player to obtain enough marbles necessary for a majority (13 in 25-A-DUB, 51 in 100-A-DUB) wins and is entitled to take in all the rest of the marbles in the ring.

A big game for big stakes, and always played "for keeps."

Big ring

A circle from three to six feet in diameter is drawn in the dirt. Then one player collects from all of the others the agreed-upon stake (usually three to five marbles each), puts them all in one cupped hand, and then quickly drops his hand away, letting the marbles fall helter-skelter into the circle.

Players shoot from the edge of the ring, the aim being to hit the target marbles out of the ring while their shooter remains inside the ring. In this game shooters are permitted to raise their shooting hands one hand-length off the ground when they knuckle-shoot. This creates "English" and helps shooters "stick" in the ring. "Roundsters" is permitted, that is, players under this procedure may move about the perimeter of the ring—as long as their distance to the edge remains the same—to get a better shooting position.

Pyramids

In this game one player constructs a small pyramid—actually a triangle flat on the ground—out of his own marbles, then draws a circle about it. His opponent (this is a two-man game) shoots at the pyramid from a designated shooting line in much the same manner as a pool player "breaks." He keeps any marble that rolls out of the ring and continues to shoot until he either misses or fails to shoot a marble from the ring.

His opponent then builds a pyramid with *his* marbles and the first builder becomes the shooter. This is billiards pure and simple.

Poison ring

In this Australian game, a concave hole is dug into the ground with a twist of the heel. This becomes the "Poison" and into it, each player puts his agreed-upon ante. Around this hole a circle is drawn which is called the "Ring."

Players bowl to see who comes closest to the ring and goes first. After this the emphasis is on shooting ability. A player must shoot a marble out of the ring, and his shooter must also leave the ring, or he has to give all of his winnings back to the "poison" pot. If he has no winnings he must pay a penalty of one or more marbles. If he succeeds in both knocking a marble out *and* getting his shooter out, he becomes "poison" and can shoot at, and eliminate, other players.

Only for the finest shooters.

Pot II

This is an adaptation of POTSIES, and not nearly as involved. A circular "pot" is drawn in the dirt, and stake marbles are placed in it. Another ring is drawn around it and this becomes the shooting border.

Players, using *scaboulders* or *steelies*, simply blast out the target marbles and keep blasting until they miss, keeping all the marbles they win. This was a Bronx game, and because it was usually played on concrete, and not dirt, it made for fast rolls and fast games.

Little ring

One of those rare games that involves both a bowler and a shooter; blasting power and shooting skill.

A small ring, about the size of a large dinner plate, is drawn in the dirt. Players put "two up" or "three up" or more into the circle, then bowl large-size marbles or *steelies* at the circle. There's a double objective: to knock out marbles (which one then keeps), to end up close to the ring, but not in it, so you can be the first shooter.

Once the bowling is finished, players switch to their shooters, usually *aggies*, and begin to go after marbles in the ring. In this game the skill lies in the glancing shot, for if your shooter remains in the ring, you are forced to return the marbles you shot out, are penalized two or more marbles (which are placed in the ring) and have to start from scratch by bowling again.

A most frustrating game.

Circle

A circle about five feet in diameter is drawn in the dirt, creating a "pot." Players put a designated number of marbles in the pot, choose by finger who goes first, then mark off a shooting area either by spanning with the hand a distance from the circle or, more commonly, by measuring two or three shoe lengths away.

In this game the object is to keep your shooter *inside* the circle and shoot the target marbles out. If a target marble is hit and comes within six inches of the perimeter, the shooter is given another try. Shooting in this game is "knuckles down."

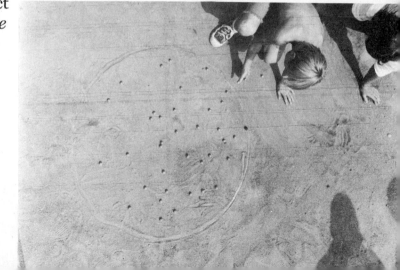

Football

In this marbles game, known as FATS in Australia, a football shape is drawn in the dirt, with a line connecting the two ends. Each player puts a marble on that line. Players attempt to knock the marbles off the line and out of the football. The game ends when all of the marbles are knocked out. The winner in this "for keeps" game is the one with the most marbles.

The player who shoots closest to the football goes first. If his marble enters the football, he shoots again from the starting line.

A Massachusetts variation uses the same figure without the center line and decrees that one's shooter is lost if it lands inside the enclosure.

Old bowler

Squares are almost as popular as circles in surface marbles games, and are known by names equally as colorful—SQUARE RING, LINEY, OLD BOWLER and SKELLEY. One of the oldest of these, OLD BOWLER, was reportedly a favorite of Abraham Lincoln's.

Draw a square in the dust with diagonal lines connecting corners. Place a marble in each corner and another where the diagonals intersect. Bowl from a starting line to see who comes closest to the square. The one closest shoots first, and plays until he misses one of the targets. The four corner marbles must be disposed of first. Then the "old bowler." Inadvertently hit the "old bowler" before the others are eliminated, and you too are eliminated!

Skelly

Similar to OLD BOWLER, but without the drawn diagonals; in addition, players can shoot from elevated positions and can shoot at any of the marbles. For a marble to be counted and kept it has to go out of the square *on the fly*, without rolling. This calls for only the best *aggie* shooters.

A West Bronx game for those with the most powerful of shooting thumbs.

Square ring

A Long Island variation in which nine marbles are placed in a drawn square. Players bowl for "firsties," then shoot "knuckles down tight" on the ground, aiming either to shoot marbles from the square or against each other to keep opponents away from the square.

A game of strategy and defense, rare in "for keeps" marbles.

Corner the market

A "for keeps" game. Each player puts a designated number of marbles in a square or a hexagon, drawn in the dirt. Often played with shooters, in which case skill is essential, but just as often played with oversized *steelies* or *scaboulders* with which the shooter simply bowls, attempting to wham target marbles out of the drawn figure.

With a good eye and a hot streak one could, in the words of the game, "corner the market" in *immies* in one's neighborhood. The *steelies* version has been favored by poorer shooters because of their blasting power.

Knuckle box

This Brooklyn variation calls for a square with 18-inch sides. Players place a specified number of marbles inside, and finger-choose to determine who goes first. The winner spans from any side of the square (tip of the thumb to tip of middle finger) to establish his shooting spot. Shooting from here, he can keep all of the marbles he hits from the square; his shooter must leave the square too. He continues to shoot until he misses or until his shooter fails to roll out of the square. It then becomes a target marble and belongs to whoever shoots it out.

Depending upon neighborhood rules, the shooting line might be one, two or three spans away from the square.

Milkie

This inversion of the general run of square game has been played on the east coast. A square is drawn and a white marble, a *milkie* of smoked glass, placed in its center. Each of the four players places his shooter outside the square, at a corner, and attempts, in turn, to shoot the *milkie* from the center of the square to any corner, without the *milkie* leaving the confines of the square.

If the *milkie* is hit to a corner, the player in that corner is eliminated. The danger is that you can come within a hair of your opponent's marble and be liable to be blasted yards away, and have to edge your way back in stages.

This is tournament stuff, with identical squares set up all over the lot, and eliminations held until there are four finalists around one square. Definitely a controlled shooter's game.

Three-and-your-own

There are just a few triangle games; two of them, KILLY and THREE-CORNER KILLY, are from Australia, a third, THREE-AND-YOUR-OWN, is from Toronto, Canada. The first two are simple shoot-marbles-out-of-a-shape games, but the third is rather interesting.

Three marbles are set down at the corners of a triangle, and a shooter attempts to hit them off the corner and out of the triangle. If he succeeds, he wins them from the player who put up the marbles stake. If he misses he loses his shooter to the triangle-maker. The triangle-maker usually wins.

It was not uncommon for a boy to come to school several hours early to stake out a particularly rough and uneven piece of concrete on which to set up his triangle. Often locations would be sold for a certain number of marbles.

For the more adventuresome, FOUR-AND-YOUR-OWN and even FIVE-AND-YOUR-OWN games were set up, though this was rare.

Persian

An indoor game. On rainy days marbles players would congregate in homes (mothers willing) which had living-room Persian rugs and enough space for some decent shooting. White thread was used to outline a portion of the rug pattern. Four players were considered ideal and the one who shouted "last!" first had the advantage of being the last to place his marbles and the first to shoot. He could set up things pretty much to his liking. This was played "for keeps"; you kept any marble you shot out of the Persian outline. A shooter's game.

Wall

Some marbles games are simply shooting games. In WALL, the player bounces his marble off a wall with the intent of hitting his opponent's marble on the fly.

War

In WAR, a player shoots, over a distance of about 14 feet, at an opponent's marble. Each time he misses, the opponent keeps the marble. If the attacker hits it, he gets the target marble and becomes "keeper of the target." Roles change back and forth and 30 or 40 marbles can be lost in no time at all.

Ho-go

Other games use marbles as tender. In HO-GO, a player holds up a hand, presumably with marbles inside, and asks "Ho-Go?" The other player has to guess how many—if any—this player has. If he guesses correctly, he gets what is in the hand. If he fails, he pays the difference between his guess and the amount held. Also called HANDY-DANDY.

Toodlembuck

Another game in which marbles are a form of tender is TOODLEMBUCK. Two sticks are needed, and a button. A circle is drawn in the dirt; in it one stick is stood on end, and the button placed on top of it.

The other stick is rolled lengthwise, on the ground, from a shooting line 15 feet away, in hope of upsetting the first stick and having the button fall into the circle. If successful, or unsuccessful, the payoffs are in marbles.

A rhyme went with this game in England and in Australia:

"Try your luck on the toodlembuck
An *alley* a shot and two if you win."

In Great Britain this game is also known as STICK-ON-SCONE.

115

Spinner

Yet another game in which marbles were but an adjunct. A two- or three-foot-diameter ring was drawn, and marbles were dropped in at random.

Each player played with a spinning top and, taking turns, would swing and release his spinner into the ring. Marbles struck and sent out from the ring were kept.

A hazard was the possibility that one's top would remain in the ring. If so it simply became another target and there for the hitting.

A run-of-the-mill spinner had about the same value as a good *aggie* shooter, so that the game led to some stiff trading.

Bridgeboard

Ho-go and TOODLEMBUCK and SPINNER—and other games that used marbles in nontraditional roles—led to the creation of games like BRIDGEBOARD. Though this game and those that follow are games of chance, most of them were ingeniously designed, with carefully computed odds and just as carefully selected materials. This English game is the earliest one we've been able to find.

A board, about a foot long, either was notched or had nails driven in along one edge to create a series of holes. This edge was stood on the ground, and players shot marbles through the holes. The shooter got whatever number of marbles was indicated above the hole through which his marble passed, or if he missed, he lost the marble shot.

This was definitely a house game, with all players desirous of being the bridgeboard man. Yet there was no shortage of players for there were dandy odds offered. This English game was among those which found its way to the United States and was improved upon with great ingenuity, as we shall see.

The first of these American adaptations we will refer to as THE CONNECTICUT VERSION. It called for a paddle-shaped piece of wood with five holes of varying sizes cut into one end. Numbers were written above these holes indicating the number of marbles to be awarded to the shooter if his marble passed through. Naturally the smaller the arch the larger the bounty. In this, as in BRIDGEBOARD, the owner of the paddle did extremely well.

The Brooklyn, New York, version, called SHOOT THE SHOE BOX, utilized a Thom McAn shoe box and its own set of numbers.

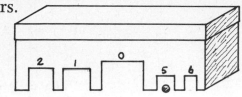

The Canadian version used a mounted board and a different set of numbers.

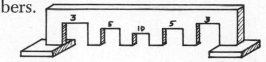

In the East Bronx they used a cigar box—preferably a Garcia Vega box, but one took what one could get—with five holes.

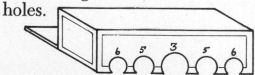

In the West Bronx, wooden Kraft cheese boxes were favored. They were smaller, could be propped against a curb, and gave the house an even better shake. Here the game was called CHICKIE NEEDS MORE CORN.

In Queens, the preference was for Philadelphia Brand Cream Cheese boxes which were long, thin and as hard to beat as a one-armed bandit. Here it was called, aptly, THE CREAMER.

Further out on Long Island, the cigar box was used. Here the proprietor on any particular day might be awarding not only marbles but perhaps candy, nuts, checkers or pennies. It was called GETTING IT INTO THE BOX, and most people didn't.

The corona

This cigar box game comes from New England. A single hole is cut into the top, and the box is rested on the sidewalk. A contestant (for that's what he is) stands upright straddling the box and drops a marble straight down in hope of getting it through the hole.

As with all "house games," all missed marbles become the property of the cigar box owner. If the marble goes in, players win as many as five or 10 marbles, depending on the customer's height and the size of the hole.

It is possible to sight, as with a gun, along one's finger down from chin height (which was the official drop level). Still it remains rather difficult to get the marble in the hole.

Boxies

Yet, another cigar box game; this from the Bronx. The box is placed upright against a curb, with the top opened back, like a ramp.

Players try to roll marbles up the ramp at just the right

speed to drop them into the box. The payoff is five to one. Care has to be exercised for if the marble is rolled too slowly, it edges off the side or slides back down; if too fast, it jumps ski-fashion over the box. As ever, the house man does just fine. An old house ploy was to use the ever-popular Garcia Vega boxes because their tops were thicker than other cigar box tops, and more often than not the marbles wouldn't make it onto the ramp.

This is known as a "clod-type" game, ideal for those who can't shoot marbles well but are good at sitting on curbs.

Prince Henry

This gambling marbles game employs a box, in this case a pyramid made of cardboard. Its apex is cut off to make a hole. From a distance of about three feet, players try to toss marbles into the hole. If successful, they collect a marble from each player.

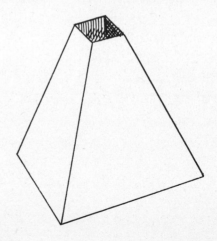

Abacus

Another "banker" game, this one from Detroit involves a line-up of strategically grouped marbles. The banker sets up the marbles in some sort of series.

Players bowl shooters at the marbles rather than shoot knuckles style. Those that are hit are won, with greatest value bestowed on single marbles standing alone.

Bowlers shoot from a predetermined point that varies depending upon the smoothness of the terrain and the values given the marbles. The higher the value, the rougher the ground and the greater the distance. Marbles that miss their mark are, of course, kept by the house man.

Sticker

A gambling game, strictly for shooters. Players shoot at a "sticker" or target marble from a shooting line some 15 or 20 feet away.

In this game, which is of New England vintage, the sticker is a highly prized *carnelian,* a superb *aggie,* or a fine oversized *glassie.* Each of these is worth about five ordinary marbles.

If a player hits the sticker, it's his to keep. All marbles that miss become the property of the sticker's owner. The owner has an obvious advantage, and can often collect several dozen marbles before his sticker is hit. With these marbles he can trade five for one and quadruple his *aggie* stock. Needless to say, everybody would want to be the "sticker." The privilege went to he who yelled "Sticker!" first. If you hit the sticker, you then had the option of becoming the house man yourself.

Dicies

Another New England gambling game, this one native to Hartford, Connecticut.

A marble was flattened on opposite sides, usually with a file, so that it would not roll and so that a die could sit flatly on top. The house man would place his target on the sidewalk or other flat area and invite contestants to try their luck.

Usually shooters were kept behind a line about six feet away. They shot at the stationary marble in the hope of jarring it with sufficient force to knock the die off. If successful they were awarded the number of marbles indicated by the fallen die. All marbles that missed became the owner's property. As usual in games like these, he did rather well. Most shooters figured this for a stacked game, but the challenge of a possible 6 to 1 was great. Those who competed were generally regarded as gutsy gamblers, an accolade probably worth a few lost *immies*.

Rockies

This Canadian gambling game (which I've called ROCKIES) is one of the most difficult, but offers a payoff as high as 50 to 1 and is therefore impossible to resist.

A single marble, usually one of your larger ones, was placed in the middle of a concrete sidewalk square. Players shot at it from a shooting line two squares away. The target square was carefully picked. Ideally it was *not* level, was not even with the next two squares, and was separated by a deep crack or a protruding ribbon of tar. Better yet, one of the other squares might have a tree root pushing it up at one end, and its neighbor be deeply cracked or pitted. The rougher the course the higher the payoff. Though the shooter virtually never won, he played.

Immie This game, a Brooklyn, New York, creation, was usually run by a fellow with an extensive collection of large, colorful and often valuable collectors' marbles which he would offer as bait.

He would sit on the sidewalk with an *immie* in front of him and offer it to whoever could hit with a shooter from two sidewalk cement squares away. Ideally the course was rough. If it was hit, it was won. The *immie* owner, however, kept all the misses.

Ostensibly it would seem the *immie* owner sat on the sidewalk to block the marble; actually he was just a distraction to the shooter.

Purees

A gambling game named in honor of the prized clear glass marbles that were the stake. In this game—a Bronx innovation—the proprietor sat on a curb, with a cigar box top in front of him, providing a backdrop for a single, prized *puree*.

Players shot at the *puree* from various distances, with higher odds given for longer shots. Thus, from six to seven feet, odds of 5 to 1 were offered; from mid-street, 10 to 1; and from the opposite curb, 40 to 1. One hundred to 1 was awarded anyone who cared to attempt a shot from the roof of a parked car on the other curb, or from a window of an apartment across the street. These bonanzas made it a lucrative game for the proprietor, who never lost.

Commies

A similar "body" game, this one created in Pittsburgh. In it, the house man sits on the sidewalk, spreads his legs wide and places an exceptionally beautiful *aggie* near the crotch of his trousers.

The players roll *commies* or cheap clay marbles at the *aggie*. A hit entitles the roller to the *aggie*, or the option of taking the house man's place. All missed marbles are the property of the *aggie* owner.

An element of tension was introduced when four or five players rolled simultaneously and then argued over whose *commie* hit the *aggie*. Girls never played this game, at least not in Pittsburgh.

Pinball

This game, popular in the 1900's, particularly in New England, is the predecessor of the modern pinball machine. It calls for a simple pinball board that could be easily constructed from a cardboard box or wooden crate. The board is propped at a slant, and marbles, held at its top, are let go. They roll down, striking nails and brads strategically placed in their path, and either fall through one of the holes or make it to the base of the board. Players whose marbles reach the numbered pockets at the bottom of the box receive the number of marbles indicated.

Most often the marbles drop out on the way, and are collected by the lucky man who owns the pinball machine.

Maurice Steele's game

And finally, gambling done with, here is the forerunner of scores of marbles-oriented games now sold in toy departments. Little skill is involved, but a player gets a lot of action for his marbles. The marble zips down three levels, emerges through a hole and hopefully hits the bell. Maurice Steele, now of Rome, New York, developed this game at the turn of the century in Hartford, Connecticut.

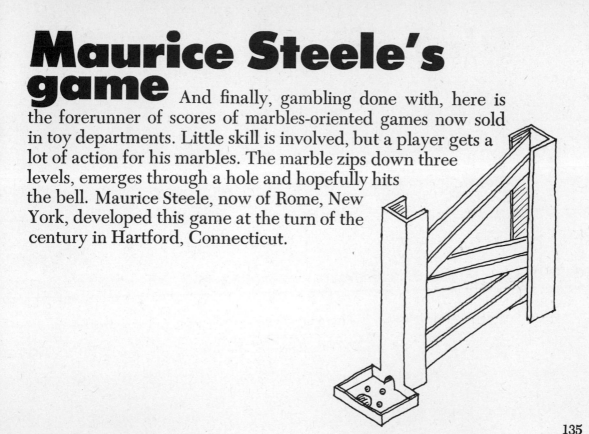

TOURNAMENTS

MARBLES BECAME an organized sport in the United States in 1922 when Macy's in Philadelphia ran off a promotional tournament of seven boys and a girl; the Scripps Howard Newspapers took over sponsorship and created an annual countrywide elimination. As the matches got underway, with attendant publicity in the Scripps Howard press, Atlantic City requested that it be the official host city for the finals. The New Jersey shore has, for the 50-year history of the National Marbles Tournament, been the locale for the finals, with the site shifting from Atlantic City to Ocean City, then to Wildwood and Asbury Park, and finally and permanently back to Wildwood in 1959. Girls have participated in the nationals—in their own division—since 1948.

The tournament, once an event of high interest, began to lose attention in the last decade. In 1968, Roger Howdyshell, President of the Marble King Company of Paden City, instituted a $500 scholarship for the national champ which has helped the tournament get through its half century.

Following are elaborate and quite rigid rules for RINGER, championship style, which is the game played in the National Marbles Tournament.

No less than two and no more than six may play in one game of RINGER, except in tournament championship matches, where only two play. All tournament play is for fair, and marbles must be returned to owners after each game.

Equipment. The playing surface shall be a smooth, level area of ground, hard clay or other suitable substances. The Ring is inscribed upon the area 10 feet in diameter, and all play within this ring. (Note: The outline of this ring shall not be so deep or wide as to check the roll of the marbles).

With the center of the Ring as a point of intersection, mark two lines at right angles to each other to form a cross, which shall be a guide for placing the playing marbles. Place one marble at the four branches of the cross, each marble three inches away from the next one.

The Lag Line is a string drawn tangent to the ring and touching it at one point. The Pitch Line is a straight line drawn tangent to the ring directly opposite to the Lag Line.

Playing marbles shall be round and made of glass. All marbles in any one playing ring must be of uniform size. The standard size shall be five-eighths inch in diameter. Slight variations may be allowed by the referee for manufacturing fault.

Shooters shall be round and made of any substance except steel, or any other metal, and shall not be less than one-half inch nor more than six-eighths in diameter, as determined by the referee.

Plan of playing. The Lag is the first operation in RINGER. To lag, the players stand, toeing the Pitch Line, or knuckling down upon it, and toss or shoot their shooters to the Lag Line across the ring. The Player whose shooter comes nearest the Lag Line, on either side, wins the Lag.

Players must lag before each series of games. The player who wins the lag shoots first and the others follow in order as their shooters were next nearest to the Lag Line. The same shooter that is used in the lag must be used in the game following the lag.

On all shots, except the lag, a player shall knuckle down so that at least one knuckle is in contact with the ground, and he shall maintain this position until the shooter has left his hand.

Knuckling down is permitted but not required in lagging. Starting the game each player in turn shall knuckle down just outside the Ring Line, at any point he chooses, and shoot into the ring to knock one or more marbles out of the ring.

A player continues to shoot when he knocks one or more marbles out of the ring—provided his shooter remains inside the ring. When a player's shooter passes outside the ring, whether or not he has scored on the shot, he shall cease to shoot. He shall be credited with the marbles he has scored.

After a miss a player picks up his shooter, wherever it lies, until his next turn, and then is permitted to take rounders and shoot from any point of the ring line.

Playing regulations. Marbles knocked outside of the ring shall be picked up by the player who knocks them out.

Whenever a marble or shooter comes to rest on the ring line, if its center is outside the ring, or exactly on the ring line, it shall be considered out of the ring; if its center is inside the ring, it shall be considered inside the ring.

If a shooter knocks out two or more marbles in a combination play he shall be entitled to all points on the shot.

When a shooter slips from a player's hand, if the player

calls "slips" and the referee is convinced that it is a slip, and if the shooter did not travel more than 10 inches, the referee may order "no play" and permit the player to shoot again. The referee's decision is final.

The game shall end when one player has knocked seven marbles from the ring.

Scoring. For each marble knocked out by a player, he shall be credited with the score of 1.

The player having credited to him the largest number of marbles at the completion of the game shall be the winner of that game.

In games where more than two players are engaged, if two or more players lead with the same score, those in the tie shall play a new game to break the tie.

A player refusing to continue a game, once it is started, shall be disqualified, and if only two players are engaged, the game shall be forfeited to the offended player.

The score of the forfeited game shall be 7-0.

Officials. The officials shall be a referee and a scorer, if a scorer is available, otherwise the referee shall also keep score.

The referee shall have complete charge of the play. He shall interpret these rules and have power to make decision on any points not specifically covered by these rules. He shall have authority to disqualify any player for unsportsmanlike conduct. He shall have authority to order from the ring or its vicinity the coach or other representatives of any player who conducts himself improperly.

The scorer shall keep a record of the game, making score of each player, shot by shot, and at the end of each game shall notify the referee of the score and the referee shall announce the winner. The scorer shall assist the referee in enforcing the rule against coaching, and call to the attention of the referee any infraction of the rules.

Penalties. A player shall *not*:

Lift his hand forward until the shooter has left his hand. This violation is known as "hunching."

Smooth or otherwise rearrange the ground or remove any obstacles. He may request the referee to clear obstructions. **Penalty** (for all these violations): If any marbles were knocked out or dislocated on the shot, they shall be restored to their place, and the player shall lose his shot.

Change shooters during the course of the game. He may choose a new shooter on each lag, provided he uses that shooter in the subsequent games. **Penalty:** The player shall be disqualified from the game.

Communicate in any way with his coach during the course of a game. **Penalty:** Forfeiture of all marbles he knocked out of the ring; said marbles to be returned to the game and placed on the cross.

A coach shall not give instructions to either his own or any other player engaged in a game. **Penalty:** Coach shall be ordered from the playing field if after being warned once, he continues this violation.

Players must not walk through the marble ring. **Penalty:** After a player has been warned for violation, the referee *may* require the forfeiture of one marble to be returned and placed on the cross.

❈ ❈ ❈

Additional rules: In lagging, players shall lag together. If either shooter strikes the backboard, or the marbles or rack in the ring, that player loses the lag. If both shooters strike an obstruction the players lag over.

Backspin: Each player shall be responsible for the results of backspin. If the shooter on its return strikes any part of the player's body he shall lose the turn, but shall be entitled to any marbles knocked out on the shot.

Marble in action: A player shall not pick up any shooter or marbles while in motion and shall not stop a shooter's or marble's motion. Violation of this rule shall be considered a foul and the player shall lose his turn.

Practice shots: A player shall not take practice or warm-up shots into the ring while a game is in progress or ready to start. Violation shall be considered as a shot. Players may take practice shots on the surface outside the ring.

Broken shooter: A Player may not change shooters during a game *excepting* that if a shooter is broken the referee may permit a change, if in his judgment the shooter has become damaged enough to impair good shooting.

Wind action: If before a shot the wind moves a marble, the referee shall return it to its original position. However, any marble or shooter set in motion during a shot shall be allowed to continue until it comes to a full stop and if the wind carries it out of the ring it shall be counted out. The marble or shooter shall be considered dead once it comes to a complete stop. If the wind moves it thereafter, it shall be returned to position.

Wrong shooter: If any player carelessly shoots with one of the playing marbles he shall lose the shot and any marbles knocked out with the illegal shooter shall be returned to position.

Picking up marbles: Each player may use his own judgment as to whether to pick up his marbles after each shot or wait until he finishes shooting, excepting any marble which bounces back into the ring must be picked up immediately.

Forfeited game: Each player shall be responsible for keeping informed as to the progress of the game. If before the actual completion of a game, a player mistakenly believes he has lost and throws his marbles into the ring he shall be considered to have forfeited the game.

Slips: The rule regarding slips shall be enforced strictly and whenever the shooter travels more than 10 inches it must be considered a shot. If a player picks up his shooter on a "slips" before it has stopped it shall be considered to have gone more than 10 inches and he loses his shot.

The lag: Players shall lag before each set of games and the winner shall shoot first in all odd-numbered games.

In tournament play there are shots to avoid and shots for which to strive. If too much pressure is put on one's shooter, the shooter may skid across the ground, off course, or bounce over the target marble. The best tourney players shoot easily, but accurately.

An important shot in tournament play is "Riding Snoogers." A snooger is a marble left near the rim of the ring. To ride a snooger is to hit this marble a glancing blow, knocking it from the ring, while bouncing the shooter into the mass of other target marbles in the center of the ring, thus paving the way for easy shots.

Following are the names of the boy and girl national champions, together with the cities and states which have sponsored them:

NATIONAL MARBLES CHAMPIONS: BOYS

1922: Bud McQuade, Baltimore, Md.
1923: Harlan McCoy, Columbus, Ohio
1924: George Lenox, Baltimore, Md.
1925: Howard Robbins, Springfield, Mass.
1926: William Harper, Bevier, Ky.
1927: Joe Medvicovich, Pittsburgh, Pa.
1928: Alfred Huey, Akron, Ohio
1929: Charles Albany, Philadelphia, Pa.
1930: James Lee, Columbus, Ohio
1931: John Jeffries, Greenville, Ky.
1932: Harley Corum, Louisville, Ky.
1933: Aaron Butash, Throop, Pa.
1934: Cliff Seaver, Springfield, Mass.
1935: Henry Altyn, Throop, Pa.
1936: Leonard Tyner, Chicago, Ill.
1937: Bill Koss, Canton, Ohio
1938: Frank Santo, Throop, Pa.
1939: Harry DeBoard, Landenberg, Pa.
1940: James Music, Huntington, W.Va.
1941: Gerald Robinson, Scranton, Pa.
1942: Charles Mott, Huntington, W.Va.
1943: Dick Ryabik, Pittsburgh, Pa.
1944-1945: No tournaments held (World War II years)
1946: Benjamin Ryabik, Pittsburgh, Pa.
1947: Ben Sklar, Pittsburgh, Pa.
1948: Herman Truman, Beloit, Wisc.

1949: George Wentz, Huntington, W. Va.
1950: Bob Retzlaff, Montgomery, Ala.
1951: Shirley Allen, Beckley, W. Va.
1952: Russell Gwaltney, Salem, Va.
1953: Jerry Roy, Huntington, W. Va.
1954: Bob Hickman, Huntington, W. Va.
1955: Ray Jones, Pittsburgh, Pa.
1956: Fred Brown, Beckley, W. Va.
1957: Stan Herold, Summersville, W. Va.
1958: Dennis Kyle, Richwood, W. Va.
1959: Mat Wysocki, Wilkes-Barre, Pa.
1960: Tom Meade, Yonkers, N. Y.
1961: Ace Millen, Yonkers, N. Y.
1962: Mark O'Mahoney, Pittsburgh, Pa.
1963: Jim Donohue, Springfield, Mass.
1964: Clarence Bower, Mullens, W. Va.
1965: Garry Malcolm, Elkhart, Ind.
1966: Melvin Garland, Pittsburgh, Pa.
1967: Barry Blum, York, Pa.
1968: Rudy Raymond, Reading, Pa.
1969: Glenn Sigmond, Wharton, W. Va.
1970: Ray Morgano,
        Penn VFW (Pittsburgh, Pa.)
1971: Rick Mawhinney, Cumberland, Md.
1972: Ray Jarrell, Whitesville, W. Va.
1973: Douglas Hager, Whitesville, W. Va.
1974:

NATIONAL MARBLES CHAMPIONS: GIRLS

1948: Jean Smedley, Philadelphia, Pa.
1949: Records missing
1950: Kay Allen, Greensboro, N. C.
1951: Ida Hopkins, Cleveland, Ohio
1952: Dorothy Hubbs, Augusta, Ga.
1953: Arlene Ridett, Yonkers, N. Y.
1954: Wanita Kuchar, Philadelphia, Pa.
1955: Karen Olson, Niles, Ohio
1956: Lynette Watkins, Philadelphia, Pa.
1957: Lois Fusco, Yonkers, N. Y.
1958: Jeanette Merlino, Yonkers, N. Y.
1959: Sandra Stefanchik, Yonkers, N. Y.
1960: Christine Zamoiski, Yonkers, N. Y.
1961: Anita Danyluk, Niles, Ohio

1962: Peggy Mullen, Pittsburgh, Pa.
1963: Patsy Coon, Philadelphia, Pa.
1964: Claudia Davis, Yonkers, N. Y.
1965: Jacqueline Izaj, Pittsburgh, Pa.
1966: Marcella Elliott, Wilmington, Del.
1967: Patricia Yurkovich, Pittsburgh, Pa.
1968: Debbie Webb, Yonkers, N. Y.
1969: Maureen Regan, Pittsburgh, Pa.
1970: Karen Yurkovich, Pittsburgh, Pa.
1971: Cheryl Elliott, Wilmington, Del.
1972: Katy Pazkowski, Pittsburgh, Pa.
1973: Debra Stanley, Reading, Pa.
1974:

CHAMPIONS BY CITIES

	BOYS	GIRLS		BOYS	GIRLS
Pittsburgh, Pa.	7	6	Whitesville, W. Va.	2	0
Beckley, W. Va.	6	0	Elkhart, Ind.	1	0
Huntington, W. Va.	5	0	Greenville, Ky.	1	0
Springfield, Mass.	3	0	Landenberg, Pa.	1	0
Yonkers, N. Y.	2	7	Louisville, Ky.	1	0
Baltimore, Md.	2	0	Montgomery, Ala.	1	0
Throop, Pa.	2	0	Salem, Va.	1	0
Philadelphia, Pa.	1	5	Scranton, Pa.	1	0
Akron, Ohio	1	0	Wilkes-Barre, Pa.	1	0
Beloit, Wisc.	1	0	Reading, Pa.	1	1
Bevier, Ky.	1	0	Niles, Ohio	0	2
Canton, Ohio	1	0	Augusta, Ga.	0	1
Chicago, Ill.	1	0	Cleveland, Ohio	0	1
Columbus, Ohio	1	0	Greensboro, N. C.	0	1
Cumberland, Md.	1	0	Wilmington, Del.	0	2

CHAMPIONS BY STATES

	BOYS	GIRLS		BOYS	GIRLS		BOYS	GIRLS
Pennsylvania	16	12	New York	2	7	Wisconsin	1	0
West Virginia	13	0	Maryland	3	0	Virginia	1	0
Ohio	3	3	Alabama	1	0	Georgia	0	1
Massachusetts	3	0	Illinois	1	0	North Carolina	0	1
Kentucky	3	0	Indiana	1	0	Delaware	0	2

NATIONAL RECORDS (SINCE 1949)

	RECORD	SET BY
Best won-lost percentage (boys)	.906	Ray Jarrell, Whitesville, W. Va., 1970
Best won-lost percentage (girls)	.925	Karen Yurkovich, Pittsburgh, Pa., 1970
Most sticks, 1st shot, preliminaries	32	Ray Morgano, Penn VFW, Pittsburgh, Pa., 1969
Most sticks, 1st shot, semis	13	Bill Sizemore, Mullens, W. Va., 1959
Most sticks, 1st shot, finals	9	Dennis Kyle, Richwood, W. Va., 1958
Best inning average (semis)	1.29	Dick Hickman, Huntington, W. Va. 1958
Best inning average (finals)	1.33	Dennis Kyle, Richwood, W. Va., 1958
Best won-lost percentage (semis)		
20 games	.900	John Gaetano, Throop, Pa., 1953
24 games	.792	Ace Millen, Yonkers, N.Y., 1961
Longest winning streak, preliminaries		
boys	27	Rudy Yakich, Pittsburgh, Pa., 1968
girls	23	Karen Yurkovich, Pittsburgh, Pa., 1970
Best won-lost record, single day	18-0	Ray Jarrell, Whitesville, W. Va., 1970
Shortest final (since 1952)	11 games to 2	O'Mahoney vs. Senita 1962
Longest final (since 1952)	11 games to 10	Brown vs. Kyle 1956
		Meade vs. Kimsal 1960
		Donohue vs. Riccardi 1963
		Morgano vs. Kokos 1970

Note: winner underlined

And lest it be thought that marbles today are only for the young on the beaches of Wildwood, New Jersey, the following proposal for permanent marbles installations at a southern country club is offered, courtesy of Oka Hester, long a National Marbles Tournament stalwart, as proof of an abiding adult interest in RINGER.

The Presentation to the Board of Directors of __ Country Club Subject: Recreation for the younger and older members

It is recommended that _____ Country Club install (initially) two outdoor and one indoor Marbles rings. Informal playing would be scheduled for Monday through Friday, with tournament play on Saturdays and Sundays, 3-5 PM (time could be altered to coincide with the cocktail hour). All contestants and the gallery would not be expected to dine in the dining room, but rather on tables set out on the porch (summer) and in the pool room (winter).

(The necessity of kneeling and the nervous tension

could produce a degree of cleanliness not conducive to the tenor of the dining room on these days.)

A. The Summer Rings. In the lighted area between the bar and the swimming pool, which is at present devoted to weeds, grass and a well worn path, two 10 ft. diameter marbles rings could be installed. They could be covered with sand or clay, but for our purposes grass would be more desirable. The golf course superintendent has always wanted an area to test various grasses for the greens and this would be ideal. The proximity to the swimming pool is excellent and access from the bar would be ideal in the event some of the older members should like to test their long unused skills.

B. The Winter Ring. Anticipating a gallery for pool players which never developed, a former recreation chairman refurbished the (then unused) basement area for a pool room. The room is 20′ x 65′ and only about a third of it is being used. I recommend that we contact the carpeting company that originally installed the carpeting and have them devise some means of marking a 10 ft. diameter Marbles Ring on the carpet for winter games. The fireplace, which does not work, could be fitted with small drawers or "lockers" and rented to those who wish to keep their marbles, knee pads, etc., right at the club.

C. Rules and Regulations. The _____ Country Club has always adhered to the rules and regulations as propounded by the PGA for golf and I suggest we follow the same procedure for marbles (i.e. use the same rules as set forth for the National tournaments). The same respect for golf rules should extend to its parent game, marbles.

D. Supervision. We have elderly members who probably know more about marbles than any of us and this would give them the opportunity to participate in more activities of the Club.

E. Summation. The greatest following of the game of marbles would most probably be those sons and daughters who are of the "forgotten age group," those who are too old for babysitters and too young to be boyfriends or girlfriends.

Normally these children of the members are left to run, shout, pout, build, break apart, swim with a passion, play clumsy tennis and if you do slip him or her by the pro for golf, they will either take 17 shots on a par 4 hole or make a hole in one and ask "What's so hard about this?" Marbles would give them an opportunity for contest in a different way.

The advantage to the other age groups is rather obvious. Where else can you get together the elderly and the young? What other game can be played by cardiacs and cantankerous children? Bridge perhaps, but who would teach the children even if they were willing to learn? In what other game could both fathers and sons (mothers and daughters) meet where each has equal opportunity and ability to compete?

In conclusion, Gentlemen, the financial outlay is minimal and the increased activity on Saturdays and Sundays should increase the revenue taken in by the dining room—*and* the bar, where an "inside gallery" could form, casual betting take place, etc.

AFTERWORD

MARBLES, we've found, is something to which people remain nostalgically attuned, no matter their age, no matter how far removed in time or distance, and we thank those who took time out to inform us:

That the late Senator Estes Kefauver once shot marbles on the floor of the Senate, and that Representative Bella Abzug was, and possibly is, great at *immies*.

That two automobile workers, desirous of helping small boys shoot big marbles, devised a sort of marbles-shooting popgun several years ago which could automate marbles games. Patent number 2,791,210.

That New York University, its football team a thing of the past, created a marbles team, "The New York Institute for the Investigation of Rolling Spheroids," and issued a blanket challenge to all comers.

That an Indianapolis woman bought her husband a bag of marbles at an auction for one dollar as a joke, and later found them to be 150 *aggies*, worth one dollar each.

That a lad in England, who watched his father "swallow" a marble as a magic feat, tried to duplicate it with 14 successive marbles and became ill.

And, finally, our thanks to Margaret Whiton, who wrote to me about a most important, and often overlooked, aspect of marbles: how they are kept and in what.

During the period that my son was devoting a lot of time to playing marbles I noticed that he spent almost as much time fondly contemplating his collection. Also it was very important that he have a container worthy of these precious beauties. This is where I came in. He was confident that I could produce a beautiful marbles bag, even though my prowess at the sewing machine had previously limited me to ordinary repair work. I remember his standing over me while under his supervision a lovely green woolen bag with silken braided cord for drawstring came to life. Then I embroidered his initials in orange. For several years this was one of his most treasured possessions.

Marbles players from Yonkers, New York. Standing, left to right: Angelo Rauso (coach), Bobby Millen, Paulette Theret, Charles Criss, Debbie Webb. Kneeling, sitting, and/or squatting, left to right: Dominick Vergalitto, Garrett Millen, Gloria Webb. Missing: Kevin Millen, who had to go home.